D1242588

Delectable Cupcakes

WITH A SIDE OF SCIENCE

An Augmented Recipe Science Experience

by M. M. Eboch

CAPSTONE PRESS
a capstone imprint

Download the Capstone app!

- Ask an adult to download the Capstone 4D app.
- Scan the cover and stars inside the book for additional content.

When you scan a spread, you'll find fun extra stuff to go with this book! You can also find these things on the web at www.capstone4D.com using the password: cupcakes.10720

Snap Books are published by Capstone Press, 1710 Roe Crest Drive, North Mankato, Minnesota 56003
www.mycapstone.com

Copyright ©2019 by Capstone Press, a Capstone imprint. All rights reserved. No part of this publication may be reproduced in whole or in part, or stored in a retrieval system, or transmitted in any form or by any means, electronic, mechanical, photocopying, recording, or otherwise, without written permission of the publisher.

Library of Congress Cataloging-in-Publication Data
Names: Eboch, M. M., author.
Title: Delectable cupcakes with a side of science / by M.M. Eboch.
Description: North Mankato, Minnesota : Capstone Press, [2019] | Series: 4D, an augmented recipe science experience | Series: Snap books. Sweet eats with a side of science 4D | Audience: Ages 9-14.
Identifiers: LCCN 2018011647 (print) | LCCN 2018021483 (eBook) |
  ISBN 9781543510768 (eBook PDF) |
  ISBN 9781543510720 (library binding)
Subjects: LCSH: Cupcakes—Juvenile literature. | Food—Analysis—Juvenile literature. | LCGFT: Cookbooks.
Classification: LCC TX771 (eBook) | LCC TX771 .E205 2019 (print) | DDC 641.8/653—dc23
LC record available at https://lccn.loc.gov/2018011647

Editorial Credits
Abby Colich, editor; Juliette Peters, designer; Tracy Cummins, media researcher; Laura Manthe, production specialist

Photo Credits
All images by Capstone Studio/Karon Dubke
Baker: Stephanie Lockling
Photo Stylist: Sarah Schuette

Printed in the United States of America.
PA017

Table of Contents

A Craving for Cupcakes

What's the big deal about these tiny treats? Cupcakes are easy to make and fun to share. You love caramel and your best friend loves peanut butter? No problem! Make some of each. You can keep them simple or make them with fancy decorations. They can be whatever you want them to be. No wonder people are passionate about cup-sized cakes!

Cupcakes also show science at work in the kitchen. The treats must rise as they bake, so they're fluffy and light. How does this happen? Ingredients mixed together create chemical reactions in your cupcake pan. The ingredients, along with the amount used, affect the chemistry. A pinch of this or a drop of that can make the difference between a delicious dessert and a frustrating flop. If you follow the directions, your cupcakes should turn out great. But understanding the science behind the baking will give you extra assurance you're doing everything right.

KITCHEN SAFETY

Follow these tips to keep everyone safe in the kitchen:

- Wash your hands with soap and warm water before you start. Wash them often while you work, especially after handling raw eggs.

- Don't taste uncooked dough if it contains eggs. Raw eggs may make you sick.

- Always make sure you have an adult help you use a knife, food processor, and other sharp objects.

- Use pot holders or oven mitts when removing the cupcake pan from the oven.

NOW HEAD TO YOUR KITCHEN SCIENCE LAB FOR SOME TASTY EXPERIMENTS!

KEYS TO GREAT CUPCAKES

All cupcake recipes require a few of the same steps. Follow these to make sure your cupcakes turn out great.

- Put a rack in the middle of the oven. Then turn on your oven and let it fully preheat.

- When you see "prepare your pan," put cupcake liners in the cupcake pan. Spray the inside of the liners with nonstick cooking spray. This will keep cupcakes from sticking to them.

- Fill each cupcake liner three-fourths full, unless otherwise noted. Do not overfill. If you have batter leftover, make a second partial batch.

- Set a timer for the lowest time mentioned in the recipe. When the timer dings, insert a toothpick or cake tester into a cupcake. The tester should come out clean or with only a few moist crumbs attached.

- After cupcakes have finished baking, place the pan on a rack and cool for 5 to 10 minutes. Then remove from the pan and let cool completely before frosting. Frosting can lose its fluffiness over time. Frost cupcakes just before serving them.

- Store cupcakes in the refrigerator for up to four days. Let them come to room temperature before serving. For longer storage, freeze the cupcakes in an airtight container for up to three months.

CONVERSION CHART

The recipes in this book use U.S. measurements. If you need metric measurements, here's a handy conversion guide.

VOLUME

1/4 teaspoon = 1.2 mL
1/2 teaspoon = 2.5 mL
1 teaspoon = 5 mL
1 tablespoon = 15 mL
1/4 cup = 60 mL
1/3 cup = 80 mL
1/2 cup = 120 mL
2/3 cup = 160 mL
3/4 cup = 180 mL
1 cup = 240 mL

WEIGHT

8 ounces = 230 grams

TEMPERATURE

325°F = 160°C
350°F = 175°C
375°F = 190°C

TIP

Do you want more information about ingredients, mixing, or frosting cupcakes before you begin? Flip to page 30. Here you'll find more information about the techniques used in this book.

Cookie Dough Cupcakes

What could be better than freshly baked chocolate chip cookies? How about putting one inside of a cupcake! These chocolate chip cupcakes have a ball of chocolate chip cookie dough in the center. As they bake, heat surrounds the outside of the cupcakes first, then works its way toward the center. The cookie dough ball bakes less than the outer cupcake, leaving it doughy. But it is heated enough to kill any bacteria, making it safe to eat.

INGREDIENTS

1 package refrigerated cookie dough
2 cups flour
2 teaspoons baking powder
1/2 teaspoon salt
1/2 cup butter, softened
3/4 cup sugar
2 eggs
1 teaspoon vanilla extract
1 cup milk
1 cup mini chocolate chips

FROSTING

1/2 cup packed brown sugar
1/3 cup confectioners' sugar
1/2 cup butter
1 teaspoon vanilla extract
1 cup flour
1/2 teaspoon salt
2 to 6 tablespoons milk, as needed
1 cup mini chocolate chips

SUPPLIES

cupcake pan and liners
nonstick cooking spray
measuring cups and spoons
mixing bowls
whisk
electric mixer

1 Roll a tablespoon of cookie dough into a ball. Repeat until you have 12 balls. Chill them in the refrigerator while you continue to work.

2 Preheat the oven to 375°F. Prepare your cupcake pan.

3 In a medium bowl, whisk together the flour, baking powder, and salt. Set aside.

4 In a large bowl, cream the butter and sugar until it is light and fluffy. Add the eggs one at a time, mixing after each addition. Blend in the vanilla extract.

5 Continue mixing slowly as you add half of the dry mixture. Keep mixing as you add the milk. Blend in the remaining flour mixture. Stir in mini chocolate chips.

6 Remove cookie dough balls from the fridge. Place one into each cupcake liner. Spoon the batter over each ball of dough, filling each liner about three-fourths full.

7 Bake for 18 to 20 minutes. A toothpick inserted into the edge of the cupcakes should come out clean. The cookie dough balls may still be sticky. Cool completely.

8 To make the frosting, place the brown sugar, confectioners' sugar, butter, and vanilla extract in a mixing bowl. Mix with electric mixer on low until combined and creamy. Add the salt and flour. Mix on medium speed until blended and creamy. Slowly add milk until the frosting is a good thickness for spreading. Use a spoon to blend in the mini chocolate chips.

9 Spread or pipe the frosting on the cooled cupcakes.

Kitchen Science

CHEMICALS RISE UP ★

Do you want chemicals in your cupcakes? The idea may sound scary, but you do! Chemical leaveners are ingredients that cause a chemical reaction in cooking and baking. Baking soda and baking powder are the most common chemical leaveners. When these ingredients are mixed into the batter, they start releasing carbon dioxide. This is the gas that creates bubbles of air inside the batter. As the cupcakes heat in the oven, the air bubbles continue to expand. These bubbles are like little balloons that make the baked item rise. As the item bakes, the dough or batter solidifies around the bubbles. The air pockets remain after the gas escapes.

Vegan Vanilla Cupcakes

Are you baking for someone who doesn't eat any animal products? You won't miss out on any flavor with these vegan cupcakes! In most baked goods, eggs add some moisture and fat. Here the vegetable oil helps make up for the lack of eggs. The nondairy "buttercream" frosting tops off the cupcake with extra moisture and flavor.

INGREDIENTS

2 1/4 cups all-purpose flour
1 cup granulated sugar
1 1/2 teaspoons baking powder
1/2 teaspoon baking soda
1/2 teaspoon salt
1 1/2 cups nondairy milk
1/2 cup packed light brown
    sugar
1/2 cup vegetable oil
2 teaspoons vanilla extract

FROSTING

1/2 cup vegan margarine
3 cups confectioners' sugar
2 tablespoons nondairy milk
1 teaspoon vanilla extract

DECORATIVE TOPPING

vegan white chocolate chips
vegan rainbow sprinkles or
    colored sugar crystals

SUPPLIES

cupcake pan and liners
nonstick cooking spray
measuring cups and spoons
mixing bowls
electric mixer
piping bag with
    small rounded tip
    or zippered plastic bag
wax paper

1 Preheat the oven to 350°F. Prepare your cupcake pan.

2 In a large bowl, stir together the flour, granulated sugar, baking powder, baking soda, and salt. In a medium bowl, blend the nondairy milk, brown sugar, oil, and vanilla extract. Pour the wet mixture into the dry mixture, gently stirring just enough to combine them. A few lumps are all right.

3 Divide the batter into the cupcake liners, filling each about three-fourths full. Bake for 20 to 22 minutes. The cupcakes should be golden brown. Let cool completely.

4 To make the frosting, beat the margarine in an electric mixer on medium-high speed until smooth, about 1 minute. Add the confectioners' sugar, nondairy milk, and vanilla extract. Beat on low until everything is combined and smooth, about 1 minute. If it's too thick to spread, add more nondairy milk, a little bit at a time. Spread or pipe the frosting on the cooled cupcakes.

5 Now make the decorative topping. Place the white chocolate chips in a small bowl and microwave for 30 seconds. Stir well. If the chips aren't completely melted, continue heating, checking and stirring every 10 seconds.

6 Put the melted chocolate in a piping bag with a small rounded tip. You may also use a zippered plastic bag with a small piece cut off of one corner. Squeeze the bag from the opposite corner to push the chocolate out of the hole.

7 Use the bag to draw designs, such as hearts or stars, onto a piece of wax paper. Drop a few colored sprinkles or colored sugar onto the chocolate while it is still soft.

8 Let the decorations cool until firm. Gently peel them off of the wax paper. Press one into the top of each cupcake, so they stand up in the frosting.

Chocolate Cherry Cupcakes

Mmm. Chocolate and cherries are so good together! This treat starts with a rich chocolate cupcake, but it doesn't stop there. A spoonful of cherry pie filling goes in the center of each. Fluffy cherry frosting tops it off. If you want even more cherry flavor, use cherry extract instead of vanilla in both the cupcake and the frosting. Your taste-testers will be cheering for cherry!

INGREDIENTS

1 1/3 cups all-purpose flour
1/4 teaspoon baking soda
2 teaspoons baking powder
3/4 cup unsweetened cocoa
   powder
1/4 teaspoon salt
3 tablespoons butter, softened
1 1/2 cups sugar
2 eggs
1 teaspoon vanilla extract or
   cherry extract
1 cup milk
3/4 cup cherry pie filling

FROSTING

1 cup salted butter, softened
5 cups confectioners' sugar
1 teaspoon vanilla extract or
   cherry extract
2 to 3 drops red food coloring
12 maraschino cherries

SUPPLIES

cupcake pan and liners
nonstick cooking spray
measuring cups and spoons
mixing bowls
electric mixer
melon baller or spoon
knife

1 Preheat the oven to 350°F. Prepare your cupcake pan.

2 In a medium bowl, blend the flour, baking soda, baking powder, cocoa powder, and salt. Set aside.

3 In a large bowl, combine the butter and sugar. Blend with the electric mixer until light and fluffy.

4 Add the eggs one at a time, mixing after each addition. Blend in the vanilla or cherry extract.

5 Add half of the flour mixture to the butter mixture and blend well. Blend in the milk. Add the remaining flour mixture and blend well.

6 Divide the batter into the cupcake liners, filling each about three-fourths full. Bake for 15 to 17 minutes. Let cool completely.

7 Make the frosting. Place the butter in a large bowl. Beat with an electric mixer until fluffy. Blend in the confectioners' sugar, vanilla or cherry extract, and food coloring. Beat until creamy.

8 Using a melon baller or spoon, scoop a small hole into the top of each cupcake. Drop a spoonful of cherry pie filling into each hole. Replace scooped out part of the cupcake over the filling.

9 Spread or pipe the frosting on the cooled cupcakes. Top each cupcake with a maraschino cherry.

Boston Cream Pie Cupcakes

Boston cream what? Boston cream "pie" is sponge cake filled with vanilla custard and topped with a chocolate glaze. People in Massachusetts think it's so good that they declared it the official state dessert. And guess what? Cupcakes make perfect miniature Boston cream pies! Simple vanilla cupcakes get added flavor and creaminess from the vanilla pudding and rich chocolate frosting.

FROSTING	INGREDIENTS	SUPPLIES
1 cup chocolate chips 1 cup heavy cream	3/4 cup butter 1 1/2 cups all-purpose flour 1 1/2 teaspoons baking powder 1/4 teaspoon salt 2 large eggs 2/3 cup sugar 2 teaspoons vanilla extract 1/2 cup milk 1 box mix vanilla pudding and the milk it requires	small pot cupcake pan and liners nonstick cooking spray small microwave-safe bowl measuring cups and spoons mixing bowls whisk electric mixer

1 Start the frosting first. Place the chocolate chips in a glass bowl and set aside. Pour the heavy cream into a small pot. Heat on the stove top until simmering. Remove from the heat and pour over the chocolate chips. Cover and let stand for 5 minutes. Uncover and stir briskly until the mixture is smooth. Cover and refrigerate for 1 hour.

2 Preheat the oven to 350°F. Prepare your cupcake pan.

3 Place the butter in a small microwave-safe bowl. Microwave for 30-second intervals, until it is melted. Set aside.

4 In a medium bowl, whisk together the flour, baking powder, and salt.

5 Place the eggs and sugar in another medium bowl. Beat with electric mixer until light and foamy, about 2 minutes.

6 Continue beating as you gradually pour in the melted butter and vanilla extract.

7 Continue mixing slowly as you add half of the dry mixture. Keep mixing as you add the milk. Then add the remaining flour mixture. Mix only long enough to combine the ingredients.

8 Spoon the batter into the cupcake liners, filling each about three-fourths full.

9 Bake for 20 to 22 minutes. Let cool completely.

10 Make vanilla pudding according to package directions. Remove cupcakes from liners. Cut off the top third of each. Spread pudding on bottom layer and replace top layer.

11 Get the frosting from the refrigerator. Whip it with an electric mixer for about 2 minutes, until soft peaks form.

12 Spread or pipe the frosting on the cooled cupcakes.

Kitchen Science

COOKING WITH HEAT

Cooking transfers energy to your food in order to heat it. This can be done in three ways:

- Conduction transfers energy directly from one solid object to another.

- Convection transfers heat through either liquid or gas.

- Radiation transfers energy through space using electromagnetic waves.

Many recipes use all three forms of energy transfer. Can you identify them in this cupcake recipe? First heat travels from the pot into the cream touching it, through conduction. Convection moves the heat throughout the liquid cream. When you microwave the butter, that's radiation. In the oven heat transfers through the air into the cupcakes. That's more convection. Heat also transfers from the cupcake pan into the batter through conduction. You can also feel convection when you open your oven and heat pours out. All these forms of energy transfer work together to bake a delicious treat you can eat!

Snowball Cupcakes

You won't want to throw these snowballs! Snowball cupcakes mix chocolate, marshmallow, and coconut. The marshmallow, added for the last few minutes of baking, spreads over the top of the cupcake as it toasts.

INGREDIENTS

2 to 3 drops red food coloring
1 cup sweetened shredded coconut
1 1/2 cups sugar
1 1/2 cups flour
3/4 cup unsweetened cocoa powder
1 1/2 teaspoons baking powder
1 teaspoon baking soda
1/2 teaspoon salt
1 cup butter, softened
4 large eggs
1 cup Greek yogurt, sour cream, or buttermilk
1 teaspoon vanilla extract
12 marshmallows

SUPPLIES

1 pint size mason jar
paper towels
cupcake pan and liners
nonstick cooking spray
measuring cups and spoons
mixing bowls
electric mixer

1 (Optional): To tint your coconut, put one tablespoon water in the jar along with the food coloring. Shake to mix. Add the coconut and shake again until completely mixed. Spread the coconut on a paper towel to dry.

2 Preheat the oven to 350°F. Prepare your cupcake pan.

3 Place the sugar, flour, cocoa powder, baking powder, baking soda, and salt in a large mixing bowl. Stir to combine.

4 Add the butter to the mixing bowl. Mix on low speed until the batter resembles moist crumbs.

5 Add the eggs one at a time, mixing after each addition. Blend in the Greek yogurt and vanilla extract. Beat everything on medium speed for 60 to 90 seconds.

6 Spoon the batter into the cupcake liners, filling each about half full. Bake for 12 minutes.

7 Remove the cupcakes from the oven and quickly place one marshmallow on top of each cupcake. Return them to the oven for 3 to 5 more minutes.

8 Sprinkle the pink coconut over the cupcakes, dividing evenly among each. Pat the tops gently so the coconut sticks to the marshmallows. Let cool completely.

Caramel All the Way

Salted caramel is a very popular treat. It's in cookies and candy, nuts and peanut butter, even popcorn and potato chips! Salt can enhance sweet flavors. Our recipe starts with a vanilla cupcake, but brown sugar gives the cupcakes a touch of caramel flavor. The filling and frosting add even more rich caramel flavor. And of course, it's topped off with salt—salty pretzels, that is!

FROSTING

1/2 cup butter
2 cups packed brown
  sugar
1/4 cup evaporated
  milk
1/8 teaspoon baking
  soda
2 teaspoons light
  corn syrup
2 cups confectioners'
  sugar

INGREDIENTS

1 batch baked vanilla
cupcakes, using the
recipe from Vegan
Vanilla Cupcakes
(pages 8–9) or Boston
Cream Cupcakes
(pages 12–13). However,
replace the white sugar
with brown sugar.

FILLING

8 ounces block-style
  cream cheese,
  softened to room
  temperature
1/2 cup dulce de
  leche (caramelized
  sweetened
  condensed milk)
1/4 teaspoon salt

TOPPING

1/2 cup chopped
  pecans
1/2 cup pretzels

SUPPLIES

heavy saucepan
measuring cups and
  spoons
mixing bowls
electric mixer
melon baller or spoon

1 Make the frosting first. Melt the butter in a heavy saucepan over medium heat. Mix in the brown sugar. Bring to a boil. Stir constantly until sugar is dissolved.

2 Stir in the evaporated milk, baking soda, and corn syrup. Bring to a boil.

3 Remove the saucepan from the heat. Let cool completely, about 1 hour.

4 Meanwhile, make your cupcakes. Use the directions from the Vegan Vanilla Cupcakes (pages 8–9) or the Boston Cream Cupcakes (pages 12–13), replacing white sugar with brown sugar.

5 As the cupcakes cool, chop or crush the pretzels. Mix the pretzels and pecans and set them aside.

6 Make the filling. Place all the filling ingredients in a medium bowl. Beat with an electric mixer on medium speed until the mixture is smooth and blended.

7 Using the melon baller or spoon, scoop out the center of each cooled cupcake. Make a hole about 1 inch (2.5 cm) deep. Place about 1 tablespoon of the filling in each hole.

8 Transfer the frosting to a large bowl. Add 1 cup of confectioners' sugar. Beat with electric mixer at medium speed. Slowly add the rest of the confectioners' sugar, continuing to mix until combined. Beat an additional 2 minutes on high, until the frosting is creamy.

9 Spread or pipe the frosting on a cooled cupcake. Immediately dip the frosted part of the cupcake into the pecan and pretzel mixture. Repeat with each cupcake.

TIP..

Place the pretzels in a zippered plastic bag. Then use a rolling pin or meat tenderizer to break the pretzels into small pieces. The bag ensures pieces don't go flying everywhere.

NEWARK P
121 HIGH ST.
NEWARK, NY 14513

Carrot Cupcakes with Cream Cheese Frosting

Vegetables in cupcakes? It may sound weird, but these carrot cupcakes are moist and delicious. Carrots add a natural sweetness to the cupcakes. In fact, carrots have been used in baked goods for centuries. They were a way to sweeten dessert when sugar was too expensive. Now you can say you're eating your veggies!

INGREDIENTS

1 1/2 cups finely shredded
   carrots (about 6 medium
   carrots)
1 cup flour
1 teaspoon baking soda
1/2 teaspoon salt
1 1/2 teaspoons cinnamon
1/4 teaspoon ground cloves
1/4 teaspoon nutmeg
2 large eggs
3/4 cup vegetable oil
1 cup sugar
1 teaspoon pure vanilla extract

FROSTING

8 ounces full-fat, brick style
   cream cheese, softened
   to room temperature (not
   low-fat or spreadable cream
   cheese)
4 tablespoons butter, softened
2 cups confectioners' sugar
1 teaspoon vanilla extract
several drops orange food
   coloring
1/2 cup chopped walnuts,
   optional for topping
green edible grass

SUPPLIES

cupcake pan and liners
nonstick cooking spray
measuring cups and
   spoons
mixing bowls
electric mixer
rubber spatula

1 Preheat the oven to 350°F. Prepare your cupcake pan.

2 If you did not buy pre-shredded carrots, shred them now. Use the smallest setting on your grater or food processor's grating attachment.

3 Mix the flour, baking soda, salt, and spices in a medium bowl.

4 Place the eggs and vegetable oil in a large bowl. Beat with an electric mixer to combine. Gradually add the sugar while beating at medium-high speed. Beat until thick, about 3 minutes. Blend in the vanilla extract.

5 Use a rubber spatula to fold the dry ingredients into the wet ingredients. Then fold in the carrots.

6 Spoon the batter into the cupcake liners, filling each about three-fourths full.

7 Bake for 25 to 30 minutes. Cool completely.

8 Meanwhile, make the frosting. Place the softened cream cheese and butter in a bowl. Use an electric mixer with a whisk attachment. Whisk on high until well blended, 1 to 3 minutes.

9 Reduce the speed to low. Add the confectioners' sugar 1/4 cup at a time, mixing after each addition. Add the vanilla extract and food coloring. Whip at medium-high for 1 to 2 minutes, until the frosting is light and fluffy. If the frosting is too thick, add 1 teaspoon of milk to thin out. If it is too thin, add a little more confectioners' sugar.

10 Spread or pipe the frosting on the cooled cupcakes. Sprinkle with edible grass.

TIP ....

Edible grass may be easiest to find before Easter. You can also find recipes to make your own, or tint shredded coconut green, as in the Snowball Cupcake recipe (pages 14–15).

Gluten-Free Cupcakes with Chocolate Chip Frosting

Chocolate and peanut butter taste great together. Yet not everyone can eat peanuts. Some people can't eat gluten (the proteins found in some grains). What's a baker to do? Sunflower seed butter tastes a lot like peanut butter. It's also safe for most people who must avoid peanuts. Plus, this recipe doesn't use any flour, so it's safe for those who are gluten intolerant. Even if you don't have allergies, you'll love the flavors!

INGREDIENTS

4 large eggs
1 1/2 cups creamy sunflower
    seed butter
1/2 cup packed brown sugar
1/2 cup granulated sugar
1/2 cup milk or nondairy milk
1 tablespoon vanilla extract
1 teaspoon baking soda
1/2 teaspoon salt
2 tablespoons lemon juice

FROSTING

1 cup creamy sunflower seed
    butter
1/2 cup butter or margarine
1 teaspoon vanilla extract
2 tablespoons cream or coconut
    cream
2 cups confectioners' sugar
1 cup mini chocolate chips

SUPPLIES

cupcake pan and liners
nonstick cooking spray
measuring cups and spoons
mixing bowls
electric mixer

1 Preheat the oven to 350°F. Prepare your cupcake pan.

2 Crack the eggs and separate the whites from the yolks. Drain the whites into a small mixing bowl and set it aside. Place the yolks in a large mixing bowl.

3 Add the sunflower seed butter, sugar, milk, vanilla extract, baking soda, salt, and lemon juice to the large bowl with the yolks. Beat everything together until creamy.

4 Clean and dry the beaters. Whip the egg whites until stiff peaks form.

5 Add the egg whites to the other mixture, a little at a time, folding them together gently.

6 Spoon the batter into the cupcake liners, filling each about three-fourths full.

7 Bake for 15 to 20 minutes. Let cool completely.

8 Meanwhile, make the frosting. Mix the sunflower seed butter and butter or margarine. Blend until creamy. Stir in the vanilla extract and cream. Slowly stir in the confectioners' sugar. Stir constantly until blended. If needed, add a little more cream or confectioners' sugar to adjust the thickness.

9 Spread or pipe the frosting on a cooled cupcake. Immediately dip the frosted part of the cupcake into a small bowl of mini chocolate chips. Repeat with each cupcake.

SAFETY TIP....................

Whenever you bake for someone with allergies, make sure to read all food labels, every time. Cross contamination is a risk for those with food allergies. Some packaged foods could be contaminated with allergens even if they are not in the ingredients.
You can also call food companies to ask if their manufacturing processes avoid cross contamination. Always be sure to clean hands, surfaces, and tools before cooking.

Kitchen Science

ALTITUDE EFFECTS

Did you know air has weight? How much the air weighs depends on where you are. Air weighs less above a mountain than it does above the ocean. The weight of the air around you can affect how cupcake batter bakes. In the lighter air, cupcakes bake more quickly. They may rise too quickly. Instead of turning out light and fluffy, they may fall flat. Baked goods lose moisture as the liquid in them evaporates more quickly. Most recipes assume the baker is close to sea level. If you live above 3,500 feet (1,050 meters), you should adjust your recipes. Look online for information about the changes you should make to your recipes.

Gingerbread Cupcakes with Cinnamon Frosting

For some people, gingerbread is a perfect winter sweet. The brown sugar, molasses, and spices seem to bring warmth on a chilly day. But that doesn't mean you can't bake these during warm weather! Anytime is a good time for fragrant gingerbread cupcakes and buttery cinnamon frosting.

INGREDIENTS

1/3 cup packed brown sugar
1/3 cup butter, softened
2 eggs
1/3 cup molasses
1 1/3 cups flour
1/2 teaspoon baking soda
1/4 teaspoon salt
1 teaspoon ground ginger
1/4 teaspoon ground cinnamon
1/4 teaspoon ground cloves
1/2 cup milk

FROSTING

4 cups confectioners' sugar
1 teaspoon cinnamon
3/4 cup butter
1 teaspoon vanilla extract
2 to 3 tablespoons milk
1/2 cup cinnamon candies

SUPPLIES

cupcake pan and liners
nonstick cooking spray
measuring cups and spoons
mixing bowls
electric mixer

1 Preheat the oven to 375°F. Prepare your cupcake pan.

2 In a large bowl, cream the brown sugar, butter, and eggs. Then add the molasses. Beat with an electric mixer on medium speed until blended.

3 In a separate bowl, mix together the flour, baking soda, salt, and spices. Blend half into the first mixture. Blend in half of the milk. Blend in the other half of the dry mixture and then the other half of the milk.

4 Spoon the batter into the cupcake liners, filling each about three-fourths full.

5 Bake for 15 to 18 minutes. Let cool completely.

6 Make the frosting. Put the confectioners' sugar and cinnamon in a mixing bowl. Stir to blend. Add the butter, vanilla extract, and milk. Beat with an electric mixer on low until well blended. Turn mixer to medium-high speed. Beat until fluffy. Add more milk if needed for consistency.

7 Spread or pipe the frosting on the cooled cupcakes. Decorate with cinnamon candies.

Peanut Butter Cup Cupcakes

Calling all peanut butter fans! This recipe is for you. A peanut butter cupcake with peanut butter frosting topped with peanuts! There's even a miniature peanut butter cup inside the cupcake. Try topping the frosting with another miniature peanut butter cup for a treat that is doubly delicious!

TIP

Replace the mini peanut butter cup with a spoonful of jelly. Add a dollop of jelly on top of the frosting. You'll have peanut butter and jelly cupcakes!

INGREDIENTS

1/2 cup peanut butter
1/3 cup butter, softened
1 cup packed brown sugar
1 large egg
1 teaspoon vanilla extract
2 cups all-purpose flour
1/2 teaspoon baking powder
1/2 teaspoon baking soda
1/2 teaspoon salt
3/4 cup milk
12 miniature peanut butter cups

FROSTING

1/2 cup peanuts
1/2 cup mini chocolate chips
2 cups creamy peanut butter
1/4 cup butter, softened
2 teaspoons vanilla extract
2 cups confectioners' sugar
1/4 teaspoon salt
1 to 2 tablespoons cream

SUPPLIES

cupcake pan and liners
nonstick cooking spray
mixing bowls
measuring cups and spoons
electric mixer

1 Preheat the oven to 350°F. Prepare your cupcake pan.

2 Place the peanut butter, butter, and brown sugar in a large bowl. Beat with an electric mixer until light and fluffy. Beat in the egg and vanilla extract.

3 In another bowl, stir together the flour, baking powder, baking soda, and salt.

4 Add half the flour mixture to the peanut butter mixture. Beat well to blend. Add the milk, beating well. Add the remaining flour mixture, beating well.

5 Spoon the batter into the cupcake liners, filling each about three-fourths full. Place a mini peanut butter cup on the top of each cup of batter. Gently press it down with a spoon until the top is just covered. Bake for 18 to 22 minutes. Cool completely.

6 Meanwhile, make the frosting. Chop the peanuts into small pieces. Blend them with the mini chocolate chips in a small bowl. Set aside.

7 In a clean bowl, mix the peanut butter, butter, and vanilla extract. Beat until light and fluffy. Blend in the confectioners' sugar and salt. Beat until everything is combined. Add 1 tablespoon cream and beat until smooth and creamy. If necessary, add the second tablespoon of cream for consistency.

8 Spread or pipe the frosting on a cooled cupcake. Immediately dip the frosted part of the cupcake into the bowl of chopped peanuts and chocolate chips. Repeat with each cupcake.

Kitchen Science

BAKE WITH SODA OR POWDER?

Baked goods become light and fluffy when the dough or batter rises. Leavening agents help make this happen. Baking soda, a natural salt, is one of these leavening agents. It creates gas when it is heated or when it mixes with acidic ingredients. Many common baking ingredients are acidic. These include brown sugar, honey, lemon juice, vinegar, and chocolate.

Baking powder includes baking soda, plus one or more acidic ingredients. Therefore, you do not need to add an acid. Most baking powder is "double-acting." It creates gas bubbles in two different ways. One reaction happens when the baking powder is combined with a liquid. The next starts when the ingredients are heated.

Almond Coconut Cupcakes

These cupcakes are like candy bars in cupcake form. The chocolate cupcakes pack a coconut punch. The frosting and topping add even more shredded coconut. A few toasted almonds proudly top the frosting.

INGREDIENTS

1 1/3 cups all-purpose flour
3/4 cup unsweetened cocoa
2 teaspoons baking powder
1/4 teaspoon baking soda
1/2 teaspoon salt
1/4 cup butter, softened
1 1/2 cups sugar
2 eggs
1 teaspoon coconut extract
1 cup coconut milk
1 cup shredded, sweetened
  coconut

FROSTING

1 cup heavy cream
1/4 cup coconut milk
1 teaspoon coconut extract
2 tablespoons confectioners'
  sugar
pinch of salt

TOPPING

3/4 cup sweetened shredded
  coconut
36 toasted almonds

SUPPLIES

cupcake pan and liners
nonstick cooking spray
mixing bowls
measuring cups and spoons
electric mixer

1 Preheat the oven to 350°F. Prepare your cupcake pan.

2 In a large bowl, mix together the flour, cocoa, baking powder, baking soda, and salt. Mix to combine.

3 In a separate bowl, cream butter and sugar with an electric mixer.

4 Add the eggs, one at a time, mixing well after each. Blend in the coconut extract.

5 Add half of the dry mixture to the butter mixture. Mix until blended. Add in half of the coconut milk and mix well. Add the remaining dry mixture and blend. Then add the remaining coconut milk and blend. Fold in the shredded coconut.

6 Divide the mixture among the cupcake liners, filling each about three-fourths full.

7 Bake for 15 to 18 minutes. Let cool completely.

8 Meanwhile, make the frosting. Place all the frosting ingredients in a mixing bowl. Beat with an electric mixer until medium peaks form, about 2 to 4 minutes.

9 Spread or pipe the frosting on the cooled cupcakes. Sprinkle each cupcake with coconut. Top with three almonds in the shape of a pyramid.

Rainbow Cupcakes

Would you like to taste a rainbow? This recipe starts with white chocolate cupcakes. Food coloring is added, and the batter is layered to create a colorful interior. The frosting is also tinted in rainbow colors. The festive results are fun to serve at parties. Or provide the baked cupcake, along with frosting in bags to your party guests. Then let them decorate their own cupcakes!

INGREDIENTS

1/2 cup butter
3/4 cup sugar
2 eggs
1 cup white chocolate chips
1 teaspoon vanilla extract
1 3/4 cups flour
1 teaspoon baking powder
1/4 teaspoon salt
1 cup milk
red, orange, yellow, green, and
    blue food coloring

FROSTING

4 cups confectioners' sugar
1 cup butter, softened
1 teaspoon vanilla extract
2 to 3 tablespoons milk
red, orange, yellow, green, and
    blue food coloring

SUPPLIES

cupcake pan liners
nonstick cooking spray
measuring cups and spoons
mixing bowls
electric mixer
12 small bowls
small (sandwich size) plastic
    bag with zipper locks

1 Preheat the oven to 325°F. Prepare your cupcake pan.

2 Place the butter and sugar in a mixing bowl. Blend with an electric mixer on medium until the mixture is fluffy. Add the eggs one at a time, mixing until just combined.

3 Melt the white chocolate chips in the microwave for 30 seconds. Stir well. If necessary, heat for another 10 seconds and check again.

4 Pour the melted chips into the batter. Add the vanilla extract. Mix for about 1 minute.

5 In a separate bowl, combine the flour, baking powder, and salt. Add to the wet ingredients and combine. Add half the milk and combine. Repeat for the remaining dry ingredients and milk.

6 Divide the batter into five bowls. They should be roughly equal, but you don't need to measure. Add 2 to 3 drops of one color of food coloring to each bowl. Mix each with a clean spoon.

7 Evenly divide the red batter among the cupcake liners. Repeat with the remaining colors. To make a rainbow, follow this order: red, orange, yellow, green, blue. When done, each cupcake liner should be about three-fourths full.

8 Bake for 18 to 20 minutes. Let cool.

9 Meanwhile, make the frosting. In a clean mixing bowl, combine the confectioners' sugar and butter. Beat on low speed until blended. Add the vanilla extract and 2 tablespoons of milk. Mix until smooth. If necessary, add the extra milk, a dribble at a time, until the frosting is spreadable.

10 Divide the frosting into five bowls. Add 2 to 3 drops of one color of food coloring to each bowl and blend well. Place each color of frosting in a separate plastic bag. Seal each bag and snip off one lower corner.

11 Top the cooled cupcakes with the frosting. Twist the top of the bag to squeeze frosting out of the hole. Make a rainbow on top of each cupcake.

Baking Help

Not sure how to do something in one of the recipes? Read here for some tips.

INGREDIENTS

• Butter and eggs should be at room temperature when you start baking. Take them out of the refrigerator about 30 minutes before you start.

• Measure ingredients properly. Use the back of a butter knife to level off the top of the measuring cup. Use a spoon to lightly sprinkle flour into your measuring cup. If your flour is packed down, you'll wind up with too much.

FROSTING CUPCAKES

For most of the recipes, you can either spread or pipe the frosting. To spread, put a dollop of frosting in the center of the cupcake. Using a butter knife or spatula, spread the frosting outward from the center. Piping the frosting provides more decorating options. A pastry bag or piping bag is designed for decorating baked goods. If you don't have a piping bag, you can use a zippered plastic bag. Fill the bag with frosting, seal it, and cut a small piece off of one lower corner. Squeeze the bag from the opposite corner to push the frosting out of the hole. Practice by piping the frosting onto waxed paper. Scoop up the frosting and reuse it. Also, cupcakes are easier to frost when they are cool or even cold. If you place the cupcakes in the freezer for 20 to 30 minutes, they will be firm enough to frost easily.

PROPER MIXING

• **Creaming** mixes sugar and butter or another fat. The fast mixing adds air until the mixture is well blended and fluffy.

• **Whisking** uses a whisk to blend ingredients together.

• **Folding** is a method of gently mixing ingredients. It's used when the mixture has a lot of air that you don't want to release. Use a rubber spatula. Run it along the side of the mixture, across the bottom of the bowl, and back up. This brings some of the mixture from the bottom up to the top. Fold the mixture onto itself. Rotate the bowl 90 degrees and repeat. Stop as soon as the ingredients are combined. Always be gentle while folding!

• **Beating** egg whites adds air. This eventually causes the egg whites to foam and then grow stiff. Peaks, or tiny points, stick up on the surface of the egg whites. First come soft peaks, where the peaks quickly flop over. With additional beating, the mixture thickens more. Medium peaks hold their shape, but the tips curl over. Stiff or firm peaks should stand straight up.

Glossary

aerate—to introduce air into a material

air pressure—the force of air pressing down on an area

altitude—the height above a certain level, especially above sea level

carbon dioxide—a colorless, odorless gas in the air that people and animals breathe out; plants take in carbon dioxide to make food; some chemicals react with heat to make carbon dioxide

chemical reaction—a process where substances undergo a chemical change to form a different substance

conduction—the transfer of heat through solid material

convection—the transfer of heat by the flow of a gas or liquid

elevation—the height above ground or another surface

energy—the ability to do work; energy exists in several forms, including heat

evaporate—to turn from a liquid into a gas

gluten—a protein mixture found in some grains and flours that helps hold dough together and makes it sticky

leaven—to lighten something, such as bread, with a substance that causes it to rise

radiation—the tiny particles sent out from radioactive material

vegan—a person who does not eat meat or any other animal products

Read More

Cook, Deanna F. *Baking Class: 50 Fun Recipes Kids Will Love to Bake!*. North Adams, Mass.: Storey Publishing, 2017.

Huff, Lisa. *Kid Chef Bakes: The Kids Cookbook for Aspiring Bakers*. Berkeley, Calif.: Rockridge Press, 2017.

Lee Heinecke, Liz. *Kitchen Science Lab for Kids: 52 Family Friendly Experiments from Around the House*. Beverly, Mass.: Quarry Books, 2014.

Internet Sites

Use FactHound to find Internet sites related to this book.

Visit *www.facthound.com*

Just type in 9781543510720 and go.

 Check out projects, games and lots more at
www.capstonekids.com